WHEN I WAKED,
I CRIED TO
DREAM AGAIN

Also by A. Van Jordan

The Cineaste

Quantum Lyrics

M-A-C-N-O-L-I-A

Rise

WHEN I WAKED, I CRIED TO DREAM AGAIN

POEMS

A. VAN JORDAN

W. W. NORTON & COMPANY
Celebrating a Century of Independent Publishing

Excerpt from "[American Journal]." Copyright © 1978, 1982 by
Robert Hayden, from *Collected Poems* by Robert Hayden, edited
by Frederick Glaysher. Used by permission of Liveright Publishing
Corporation.

For information about permission to reproduce selections
from this book, write to Permissions, W. W. Norton & Company, Inc.,
500 Fifth Avenue, New York, NY 10110

For information about special discounts for bulk purchases,
please contact W. W. Norton Special Sales at
specialsales@wwnorton.com or 800-233-4830

Manufacturing by Versa Press
Book design by Daniel Lagin
Production manager: Julia Druskin

ISBN 978-1-324-05093-3

W. W. Norton & Company, Inc.
500 Fifth Avenue, New York, N.Y. 10110
www.wwnorton.com

W. W. Norton & Company Ltd.
15 Carlisle Street, London W1D 3BS

1 2 3 4 5 6 7 8 9 0

For Bessie Jordan

Contents

SUCH SWEET THUNDER

WHEN I WAKED, . . .

IRA ALDRIDGE WAS HERE

here among them   the americans   this baffling
multi people   extremes and variegations.   their
noise   restlessness   their almost frightening
energy

—FROM "[AMERICAN JOURNAL]" BY ROBERT HAYDEN

BE NOT AFRAID; THE ISLE IS FULL OF NOISES

For I am all the subjects that you have.

—CALIBAN, IN *The Tempest*,
BY WILLIAM SHAKESPEARE, ACT I, SCENE 2

SYCORAX

Hex

The day of the spell was the day of cast shadows,
of diaphanous figures whipped clean of fear,
angels ablaze sailing a coastline of hushed tête-à-têtes,
adagio tenor wails laced with rage, smoke rising
from the wails, from the laughter; just when
the last local trains crawled into stations;

just when televisions grew verdigris in homes, obsolete
from indolence; just when Black signatories erased
their names and put on their boots, cirrus streaks formed
on the skyline of the city. A mother held her
barely alive son, the son to whom she vowed
protection from harm. Having thrown a circle

of goofer dust to enclose her enemies, she raises
a totem over her head. It's now time: Let her wield
the words of Black declensions, new vowels,
the best nouns of home training, of damn good sense.
Let her sit for a spell, wipe sleep from her eye.
Let her obtain a license for what's lethal

from whatever God has taken her image,
whenever the sun comes over the buildings,
whenever the moon weighs more than the sun,
more than Pisces and Neptune. Walk to
a street corner with plenty of witnesses,
where you'll bear no isolation,
sing your words facing North or even higher.

Now, walk backward through the chains
of time from each past and current hindrance
to our future. Invoke the names of those
not ceding privilege in boardrooms, the ones who oppress
to their graves. Now summon each forgotten spirit,
each fallen son. Bless each prayed-up grandmother,

each open door and vivid corridor. Bless the pains
spared you, vicarious to you, passed down in your blood,
carrying you through the dangers and the echoes of time.
Remember: family echoes within your body; history
pulls through you as you move through a day.
Raise them in this . . . prayer, let's call it,

to that God who took your image.
Go to the tree, to the home, to the street corner,
and spread these words—tossing wreaths,
spinning incantations—where torn
life collapsed under a last breath.

CODE NOIR,

OU

RECUEIL D'EDITS,

DÉCLARATIONS ET ARRETS

as·ter·isk| ˈastəˌrisk | *noun* a symbol (*) used to mark printed or written text, typically as a reference to an annotation or to stand for omitted matter. Before George Peele's play *The Battle of Alcazar*, some scholars believe the first Black actors appeared in Christopher Marlowe's *Tamburlaine*, but because they didn't have speaking roles, we don't have the names* of the actors. ~ Until his death at the hands of police, Philando Castile* worked for the Saint Paul Public School District* for fourteen years. ~ Sandra Bland* went to Prairie View A&M University on a marching band scholarship; she played trombone. She was arrested "on suspicion of felony assault on a public servant,"* after a white cop pulled her over for failure to signal while changing lanes. When she was found dead in her holding cell at the Waller County Jail, held on a five-thousand-dollar bail, no one mentioned her music.

A PARIS,

Chez les LIBRAIRES ASSOCIEZ.

M. DCC. XLIII.

Tamir Rice Case

On November 22, 2014, when officers Timothy Loehmann and Frank Garmback arrived at the Cudell Recreation Center's gazebo, driving their squad car on the grass directly in front of the picnic table at which Tamir Rice sat, Tamir got up. Seeing a police car coming in hot, at high speed, driving on grass in the middle of a park and barely coming to a stop in front of you, who wouldn't get up from their seat? Initially, the report said that the officers shot within two seconds of seeing Tamir. But if you watch the video, as I have many times now, you'll see that the car hasn't settled to a stop before Tamir is shot. Later, it's revealed that they shot him less than two seconds after pulling up.

The timing of the killing is important. An argument made about the shooting—an argument that allowed the officers to justify their shooting—is that the Airsoft pellet gun Tamir was carrying looked a good deal like a real Colt M1911 semi-automatic pistol, but this would only be important if Tamir had a chance to pull out the toy and if the officers had time to see it and to assess whether it looked lethal. If you shoot someone before they have a chance to resist or to pull a weapon or to issue a threat, are you really killing them because you feel threatened? What, then, could you be threatened by, seeing a twelve-year-old Black boy standing in front of you?

Airsoft

Like a whisper from a friend
telling a secret, the gun
reveals itself only to invite—

not start any trouble, mind you,
just to invite—the boy
who listens to come out to play.

And the boy knows not so much
what the gun's pellet says
as he understands what the pellet

will mean to say, whistling
through a windy afternoon
past onlookers who neither hear nor see

the streak of inhuman
intent searing through the ether,
so he takes his Airsoft pellet gun in hand

as he might take his laces in hand
to tighten them more securely
around his juvenile ankles—

that's to say, without much care,
but just out of habit before taking off
to run; everyone runs faster

with tight laces. This makes sense,
of course, and the hope to run can excite
as much as hitting full stride with wind

washing over a boy's face.
And toy guns masquerade as lethal guns
in a boy's dreamland where no one dies,

where they simply lie down and play dead,
but they live to play on.
As mysterious as a cat in a box,

a toy gun in a Black boy's pocket,
the gun neither dead nor alive,
unless offered a chance to empty

his pocket to solve the paradox
of what a day might hold.

Fragments of Tamir's Body

. . . I am dead.
Thou livest; report me and my cause aright
To the unsatisfied.

—HAMLET, IN *Hamlet*, BY WILLIAM SHAKESPEARE, ACT 5, SCENE 2

     the body's shadow
had much to say,
but no one in earshot
understood its language

※

     the clouds stood heavy,
and when the cops confronted the body . . .

※

     the boy showed his prowess to indulge in play,
just one of his many gifts,
which scared onlookers

※

     no Black man appeared in the park,
just a child, just people judging him

＊

as he approached,
she wondered how she'd explain him
to her father

＊

the opportunities for joy
presented themselves
in more colors than the boy
could name, so he chose Black,
enjoying them all

＊

passersby who laughed at him
showed their gratitude by memorizing his face,
then by wielding his visage whenever
they found themselves in a jam

＊

was his laughter a declaration
of his joy or a sacred prayer
offered over poor souls resigned to their fate

＊

corn chips, black licorice, marbles,
plastic pellets, toy gun, jaw breakers,
bubble gum: crushed apogee of memory

*

when he imagines knowing then what he now knows,
he imagines dying before his time

*

a jar of preserved pears,
canned by his grandmother,
occupies his mind. When he gets home . . .

*

a man beats a drum in courtship to his beloved . . .
nah, a boy dribbles a basketball,
boasting of his youth

*

a saga took place in the mind of the police,
as they glimpsed the Black child,
who was caught smiling as he walked toward them

*

his sister's scream, pulled
from a well too Black to ring shallow,
echoes whenever his name . . .

Bored, Tamir Chooses to Dream

Well, once a path is chosen, there's no limit
        to where you might arrive. Imagine his playing,
high above layered rooftops and along the edges

of trees; at one point, following the curving line
        of the skyline or the grade of the grass;
at another, the invisible whims of the breeze.

Imagine him sheering off as soon as the range
        of the city's rooftops disappears and deciding
here, *here is where I'll drum, here is where I'll*

play the cop and the robber, and here I'll
        fall asleep like a bird, tucked head under wing,
a world of limbs and leaves to support me.

Once a boy dreams, there's no limit
        to where he might soar off, above
pointing fingers and straining voices

trying to name his species. A boy
        like that would seek a laughter
loud enough to reach him

above anything pointed at him,
        above anyone approaching him,
above any sound thin enough to pass

through the gossamer of his dreams
        and just disappearing into a murmur
below him too faint to offer a reason

        to look at what could possibly disturb
the object of his day.

A Tempest

Dead or alive, she was my mother, and I won't deny
her! . . . I respect the earth, because I know that Sycorax is
alive.

—CALIBAN, IN *A Tempest*, BY AIMÉ CÉSAIRE, TRANSLATED BY
RICHARD MILLER, ACT I, SCENE 2

Of course, there's the rain, the wind, its trance of a storm over
the susurrus of people getting on with their lives, the burden-
some carrying of their souls on their backs. The mother of
the deceased son is there with the tattoo of her son's face on
her shoulder, the tattoo that survives longer than her son did.
And, of course, there's also the mother who still has the son—
barely alive—after the trauma of the storm, its rain falling
like a shroud over the dead. Both mothers always dread these
moments of transition, waiting for storms to pass, later tak-
ing inventory either of the loss or of what survived.

Waking within the home still owned by the bank, or within
the home in which rent's due to the landlord, she tries to
carry on. Now, she lives in a place she worked to maintain to
hear the movement of loved ones alive and well, but, instead,
she—that mother who lost her son or that mother whose son
survived a trauma—hears the ghost of youth in the home. But
how does she go on? Why work to keep this structure that can
no longer be a home?

Now, turn to another mother, one who has a newborn son and observe: Beneath her hands, she shields the boy's head from the rain, the head dappled by the drops moving in between her fingers, all the exposed skin the parent can't seem to cover from the storm. It's not the beauty of this moment we're to pay attention to but the beauty of its evanescence. These moments, fleeting even in reverie, will haunt beyond this moment.

Surrounding the mother and the son, the storm, however you define it in your life. Rattling shuttered windows, threatening the glass of those windows, driving the violence of outside into the home; and, if caught outside already, it drives people to shelter; if divined, they make it home; if less fortunate, they get pinned under an archway, or nestled into a plexiglass bus-stop shelter.

The storm discourages people from taking steps to walk their path. It finds every dry comfort of the body and every crevice worthy of fetish: it drips into the small of the back, the crook of the armpit, the interstices between the toes and settles there and there and even between there, reversing a pleasant stroll to a slog of life. But it's just a storm, one may say, whether of rain or of a trauma a storm will pass. Storms prey on a moment in a life, a moment that makes a soul self-conscious of the body in which it's housed.

A Window into Caliban

	Known to Caliban	**Not Known to Caliban**
Known to Others	*For learning me your language,* a plague I purge from my mouth with invention, and you know because I told you so. In plain view I reveal my charms whether you accept them or not.	They fear his memory of himself before there was a him. If awakened, he might know *I have used thee.* If of use to me he is of no use to himself, which is another kind of monster.
Not Known to Others	I remember more than I tell others, including my birth. In the first place, I don't trust easily, being Black and comely, but in the next 'cause my mother taught me better. When a body endures pain a long time without reprieve, one first grows numb but then grows wise.	There's a Blackness so deeply committed to its hue that light cannot escape its pull.

Vestiges

I would like to swim in the Atlantic,
to swim with someone who understood
why my fear of drowning plays less dire
than my fear of bones, walking the ocean floor.
I would like to sync my stroke with a beloved.
I'd like to stand on deck on a boat
and jump in the sea and say, follow me,
and know you would. The sea is cold
and it's deep, too, I'd joke,
standing at the edge of the boat's bow.
A wind breathes across the sea,
joining gently the edges of time.
With a dog paddling behind me,
I want to crawl across the water
without thinking about a future.
I have set my eyes upon the shore
and I hold you there—steady, in focus—
but let you go when, from below,
a voice breaks to the surface.

SYCORAX

How Far Away Is Caliban's Light?

Those lights filling the back window
of the car create the shadow, create
the paranoid night air, the waning moon
as it hovers above the car. Yes, it's a sin,
but I do worry. The figure my son strikes
when he encounters cops, who hold either fear
or contempt in their eyes—both useless—
brings not what you'd expect. Strangely
not anger, but clearly, not love either:
My son simply wonders will he be seen.

Imagine a deer walking a yellow line
at an hour as dark and as still
as the sheen of the deer's hide in the night,
a car swerving away, but not quite
fast enough, and then the car
and the deer meet. You see, a deer will
go on staring a threat in its eyes, and
unyielding cars will hurt themselves.

The questioning of who was in the wrong,
always seems the wrong question; assigning
blame to a light so far from its body—

a body neither named nor understood,
lying in the middle of the road.

In such moments, one must ask
if you're more deer than car;
some think the deer dumb but deer
merely defy, accepting their consequences
standing for what they believe in,
their right to see even when not fully seen.

A Window into Sycorax

	Known to Sycorax	**Not Known to Sycorax**
Known to Others	My Caliban, still in his onesie, posed a threat. Perhaps it was his hands, much too large for a newborn, which made him look like a grown man. His frontal lobe stuck out, heavy with thoughts. His eyes wide open, he looked around as if he could see auras of others who kept their thoughts to themselves.	She will never be accepted among us.
Not Known to Others	Because I saw a crow in the sky. Because the moon didn't show its face. All of time divides between my loves and my regrets. That's why I know. That's why you're just guessing. How far did the thread unspool as it led me down the path back home? Yes, a thread unraveled my coat, all the way here. It was cold when I started; it was temperate once I stopped. How many heels have I worn down on my journey? I remember a future as if I had been here before; my mother said I had been here before; now, finally, I believe her as I look into the face of my son.	How she drifts in dreams she has yet to discern. How the wind calls when she's in danger, trying to warn her of lies falling as blithely from mouths as leaves from trees. How a man will look over his shoulder to watch her walk past him on the street; she never looks back at him. She's not curious about a *him*. Why she forgets the bewilderment of hope once experience consumes her . . . Who knows? No time to ponder when life calls you to do.

SYCORAX

"Mother to Son"

My dearest, my fortune, my carrier of memories and convoluted ideas and music I plant within you like a seed to bear fruit in years to come, while the wind carries us and the sun warms us and the torpid clouds drift under the moonlit sky, while the newspapers carry our history as we live it, while you begin, even now, to form your opinions and understand the truth of yourself in the world and I am hobbled by single motherhood and the gossip that follows, while you encase in my womb, free in this pool of history that you will not remember, you will intuit our connection, long after I am gone, we will cover the distance, guided by the stars and their signal from epochs past, and you'll continue shining, long after my temporal light has doused.

A Window into Prospero

	Known to Prospero	Not Known to Prospero
Known to Others	All day, I peruse the land, the roads leading to dreams, and waters outlining fortunes, people who die in the middle of all comings and goings, living, trying to live, among the thistles of plants and the persistence of weeds. On either side of this isle, the dead soon are forgotten, the living are as casual as the dead, all eyes and gestures, tourists with suitcases open for fun, inhabitants waiting for visitors, promising only promises.	Prospero saunters past, leaving opportunities in his wake. Caliban picks through the debris, the debris of moments of aggression, tethered to his fate, but Prospero, nose in the air, stays his path unaware of the destruction left behind. Caliban and his friends, all aware, huddle in the streets. Then, if just for a moment, Caliban's and Prospero's eyes meet, a recognition builds from fear from one and from suspicion from the other, but they soon look away. Only one knows what he must do to survive.
Not Known to Others	Not simply the idea, but a real book of knowledge fits my hand like a mitt. When my world looks at me, I feel, feel in my body, like the first blossom on a tree in my backyard. This beauty belongs to me, growing and reaching upward, spreading its seed across the land. And where people exist, they are mine, whether my brethren or my children.	The world is changing around him, slowly, like drops of water on stone, drying in the sun after a rain. Millions of years ago, the area in Sedona, AZ, known as Boynton Canyon was fully underwater. Now, fully exposed, it's a destination for hiking. The world works in this way.

PROSPERO

A Tempest in a Teacup

Assume, just for a moment,
I am denied a job
in the factory of my dreams
under the fluorescent lights
of a porcelain white foreman.

It's orderly and neat.
I feed my family.
No one questions my face.
I raised my son in my likeness,
so he would never go unseen,

bobbing on a wave of expectation,
I set in motion with my back
put into my work, praying
for my country, blessed
with more of me, never worrying

about those who might die,
or those who did, trying
to stir a storm, trying
to stand where I'm standing.

Sycorax Blues

One might call my fleeing expatriation, but it simply was a psychic vacation, a way to free the mind to allow the body to follow suit. Then, just as I came to feel good about myself, my seducer said, "You won't make it out there," as I waved goodbye, already beyond his reach. A hand waving goodbye. One of those gestures read, from the distant gaze of an observer, either as great sadness or quiet ecstasy, either the tearful end or a fresh beginning. From a distance, one never knows whether the observed simply needs a bit of time away or if they are, in fact, escaping some oppression. All of these can be true within the one who waves the hand. In that sense, a good goodbye should begin with a yearning. Even at the outset, the desire either to return to another, or, just as easily, to get beyond the grasp of another can come from within us—springing from the same neuroscience of the body. Escaping can be as intoxicating as the initial longing to couple with another.

※

Now, I will try to explain my reasoning for my departure—should I call it a *departure* or an escape, even though I never fully succumbed to bondage?—here in these pages, and I will try to explain my decision to return to Algeria, fearing I may not have the luxury to explain to my child by the time he can make sense of my tongue, from which springs the various languages of a citizen of the world; nonetheless, here I try.

For two nights the wind blew from the south and trees bent over defeated like epiphanies on the faces of old men. The townspeople got up the next morning to head to their factories, to tend to their crops; children headed off to school, but roads were covered with tree branches, with stones, and with trash everywhere. Roofs were lifted off shingled homes. The air smelled of coming rain, which brought more fear: rain with the wind would be the end of this world. Just imagine, all of this, such a large hand from the sky to pluck one child from my breast.

To spare the town, I decided to leave that morning.

The Devil that he was, he had no power over the sea. He watched me sail away, unable to do anything about my waving hand. The baby cried as soon as we took to sea, and I knew my baby felt free, full of pleasure. He felt the town stretch farther from him. When we passed the first buoy, I heard the ship's whistle blow, felt it deep in my belly. *Be not afraid, dear child*, I whispered, *the island is full of noises. Sleep. Dream.*

❋

You are many women, Prospero said. I knew this to be true, but not in the tone in which he uttered the words. Indeed, many women live within me; many people live within me. The Self and the Other live within me. He wanted all of my selves and needed each one, sometimes one at a time, sometimes more than one at a time, but he could never handle all of us. There's the rub.

*

Time passed. Someone brushed the back of my neck. I writhed up, becoming a wind myself, and I flowed out the window of my bedroom. Maybe I also emitted a moan over the croaking of the frogs in the night. Then I raised my arms to the clouds, rooting my feet deep in the soil. A stretch, I called it.

Now I was pure nature in the night, still too young to worry about men. I opened my nightgown but offered nothing to anyone. *This is for me*, I said aloud to the night. Without my clothes I was a world of possibility, more than a desire. I, knowing better, I ought to mind my place, I ought to walk like a lady, I ought to mourn him when he is gone. People would have laughed had they seen me out their windows, naked but for my open nightgown flapping like a flag: I was small, but the conviction of my stance would have made me seem immense through their windows.

And for my last spell, I disappeared from his grasp, but just as the last essence of my being slipped away, he—somehow beyond my scope—caught hold of his son.

sus·pect *verb* | səˈspekt | *[with object]* **1.** have an idea or impression of the existence, presence, or truth of (something) without certain proof: As in, If she *suspects* he's dangerous, she may clutch her purse a little tighter, as she passes him on the sidewalk. | *[with clause]* : She *suspected that* he came from the other side of town; he *suspected that* she thought he wasn't from around here because he didn't look like her. Neither being sure of the other, she called the police, *suspecting that* they'd look into it. • believe or feel that (someone) is guilty of an illegal, dishonest, or unpleasant act, without certain proof: As in, A man *suspected of* armed robbery fit the description: Black male, 5 feet 9 inches to 6 feet; 20 to 40 years of age; 150 to 200 pounds. **2.** doubt the genuineness or truth of: He provided both his license and registration, but the officer still said he had reason *to suspect* stolen cash was in the car.

noun | ˈsəsˌpekt | a person thought to be guilty of a crime or offense: After getting a tip that he might be in the area; after apprehending him, after forcing him to the ground and tasing him, as he tried to run away; after he explained how they'd made a mistake; after he provided his alibi; and after hours of questioning him, the police arrested the *suspect*.

SUCH SWEET THUNDER

Malick Sidibé's photographs enable us to revisit the youth culture of the 1960s and our teenage years in Bamako. They show exactly how the young people in Bamako had embraced rock and roll as a liberation movement, adopted the consumer habits of an international youth culture, and developed a rebellious attitude toward all forms of established authority . . . To the youth in Bamako, Malick Sidibé was the James Brown of photography: the godfather.

—MANTHIA DIAWARA, "THE 1960S IN BAMAKO: MALICK SIDIBÉ AND JAMES BROWN"

Robin Taylor, photo of Malick Sidibé's studio, Bamako, Mali, July 2004

A Midsummer Night on the Town in Bamako

We all have our heroes. We all have someone who we've admired to a point of mimicry, even if it was only for a fleeting moment in our youth; we all have been in that moment when we wanted to talk like, walk like, or dress like someone we thought was cool. Fashion, music, sports—they're all informed by this desire, and they all inform what we desire. In the 1960s, in Bamako, the capital of Mali, photographer Malick Sidibé chronicled that desire.

The youth of Bamako got hip to western music and western fashion, and a cultural revolution began to emerge, although it was mostly clandestine, relegated to after-hours spots and dance halls, or simply buried in one's heart. Nonetheless, much to the chagrin of the more traditional generations that came before them, generations predominated by Islamic beliefs, the youth started listening to The Beatles and dancing to James Brown and young people wanted to dress the part and to move to the music. For their elders, though, the influx of western culture was not cool.

If you're growing up in America—pretty much at any point on the timeline of America, if you think about it—there's no moment when your culture is so protected that you'd have to strategize to bring another culture into your world. The struggle for African Americans has been to hold on to any vestige of an African culture, and I'm talking from 1619 to

today. Any African cultural influence was/is systemically—
and, at times, physically—beaten out of us.

When filmmaker Cauleen Smith approached me in 2006 to
collaborate with her on a project using Sidibé photos, I didn't
know who Malick Sidibé was. She explained what was hap-
pening in Bamako in the 1960s, and the more I read about it,
the more it reminded me of my youth in Akron, Ohio, in the
1980s when I was obsessed with Prince. I completely related
to the teens of Bamako, sneaking out of their homes to listen
to music that wasn't played on the radio and to dance at a
party that no adult knew about. There were no cell phones,
no phone trackers, no text messages. News of the party trav-
eled by word of mouth, if you were cool enough to get the
word. So, you had to have your clothes and your hair ready
to go. For me, unfortunately, it was a moist Jheri curl and
always something purple on hand.

But I digress. Cauleen, already an award-winning filmmaker
who had shown to acclaim at the Sundance Film Festival—
check out *Drylongso* or *The Fullness of Time*, my favorite
sci-fi film, period!—had received a grant from the Fluent-
Collaborative Testsite in Austin, Texas, and she asked me if
I'd like to partner with her on this project. We were both on
faculty at the University of Texas at Austin. There weren't
many faculty of color at UT Austin at that time—I was the
first African American male to receive tenure in the English
Department, and that was in 2006—and there were fewer

African American faculty who were artists. We quickly became friends.

Collaboration is a form of translation. You have to figure out the language of the other artist as you bring your language together with theirs. In this case, I firmly believe that poetry is a visual art form, so there's a natural discourse between film and poetry. I think of it more like translating Portuguese into Spanish; much of the language looks and sounds alike. The films of Cauleen Smith have a particular logic akin to a lyric poem. We'll notice a lyric movement—sometimes the sound of one scene bleeding into another, an image of one scene associating with an image in another, sometimes an exterior action rhyming with an internal thought—that forms a constellation of understanding that both surprises and, yet, still feels logical. Often, the images in her films are not only from a Black diasporic iconography but they also come from the even broader canvas of the Black imagination. All that to say, beyond our friendship, I trusted this filmmaker to shoot scenes based on poems.

But this is a three-way collaboration. And I think we both felt a duty to honor the impetus behind this project: the photography of Malick Sidibé. He, indeed, is the godfather of this collaboration. With that in mind, I think a new, distinct language was formed in the making of the film, *I Want to See My Skirt*. I was pushed to write faster than I've ever written before, so I felt the need to establish structure early and so decided to use a good deal of form here, mostly sestinas, which, with the repetition of the six chosen words, works like a weave in a textile. Sestinas have a mathematical weaving of chosen words that offers many options within strict parameters; it's like a teenager finding freedom under the rules of her parents' home. I thought a great deal about the weave of the tailor, helping these young people feel closer to their heroes; and I thought about the weave of the more traditional garb of their parents, the mud cloth of the pagne skirt or the boubou tunic; and I thought about the weave of our three artforms coming together to make a new tapestry, something agile enough to hold the past and the present close to our hearts, while also allowing us to hold on to a culture that at once feels both distant from our personal experiences and, strangely, exactly like our shared experiences.

ju·ve·nile| ˈjo͞ovəˌnīl, ˈjo͞ovən(ə)l | *adjective* of, for, or relating to young people: As in, *juvenile* love. • childish; immature: Shango's bored and begins his *juvenile* plans. / He wants the attention of Rokia, his *juvenile* crush. / Some see a walking *juvenile* crime, but she sees more, the makings of a man. • of or denoting a theatrical or film role representing a young person: In the movie in his mind, she's the *juvenile* lead. Other boys just hush. / In the movie in her mind, he's the juvenile lead. He'll soon see. / In the movie in their minds, they're a *juvenile* couple. The scenery? Lush.

• *noun*, a young person: The *juveniles* sneak out at night, so adults can't see. / Shango looked him in the eye: "*Juvenile*, maybe, but never call me boy!"/ Just a young Black male & a young Black girl, *juveniles*, living free.

• Law, a person below the age at which ordinary criminal prosecution is possible (18 in most countries): They call it a crime, sentencing a *juvenile* just for dancing to James Brown, just for expressing joy. / The police throw teens around, spitting, "*Juvenile* delinquent," as the club comes down. / When the courts say, "He'll be tried as a *juvenile*," the gavel knows his future's destroyed.

Cauleen Smith, still from *I Want to See My Skirt*

Rokia Discusses Her Photo as Girl in Skirt

It's the eyes, not the clothes that reveal
the most in my photographs, and this one
in particular. Already topless, subversive,
flip-flops and that linen skirt, hand on hip,
hoop earrings and all, everyone
should have seen the woman
in me coming of age.

At once, the young woman—
me, age 7—in this photo looks like a child
who might be in a hallway in her school;
in front of her classroom, on a Friday;
or on her way to enjoy youthful curiosity.
But look again in her eyes,
and one might see the look of a woman,
me, after a full workday, after conflict with a boss,
after the last hope for play has begun to dim.

Notice the tiles leading nowhere on which I stand.
Notice the eyes are guided toward the beyond,
as if I'm looking past my observer,
which one may interpret as rude. One might
also interpret this as a look of desperation,
need, or despair. Think of these eyes as a photo
inside this photo of the aftermath of three
hours in some church. These eyes know nothing

of parties after dark or laws against nudity,
only a chance to do her part for her family.

The eyes stare as distinct, luminous guides inside
the house or the town; guiding like two dogs
leading us through her day, in weighted steps
falling and rising like the day's light that beams
and weakens in the same instant; beating
the odds of her frailty; knocking on doors;
passing the time with dreams; seeking
light on the other side of walls.

Rokia's Parents

MOTHER

In her skirt, she looks like a woman who understands
the power of accessories. No shoes, no top. No problem.
I love watching her love herself. The emperor's clothes
were a problem because he couldn't appreciate his body.
But a child knows better. She has full knowledge
of the gift the skin gives to the skirt.

FATHER

It's not so much the flare of the skirt
that worries me. You must understand,
though, from a man's perspective, knowledge
of what a woman has beneath a dress can be a problem,
if you don't have a sense of what the body
can do when not covered by the tailor's clothes.

MOTHER

Who're you? Jomo Kenyatta? ". . . covered by the tailor's
     clothes."
She's four! She's excited about her first skirt,
man. She doesn't know anything about her body
other than she likes fashion. Don't you understand
that this is a woman's prerogative, not her problem.
Her first lesson: a woman learns her skin's knowledge.

FATHER

Remember, she's four. Does she need to possess knowledge
of the flesh? There's nothing wrong with her liking clothes,
but I don't want her thinking it's no problem
to walk around nude with nothing more than a skirt
from the States. Don't forget, I, too, understand
the ways of the flesh and the power of the body.

MOTHER

Of course, I don't want her having full power of her body.
Not that there's always danger in the knowledge
a child has with something new. She only understands,
intuits, there's a change in the world through clothes.
Let's not make such a big deal over a skirt.
When I put it on her, it was for fun: not a problem.

FATHER

Yes, my dear, trust me, it's not a problem.
But a father must show concern for his daughter's body.
There's no reason why I should skirt
around this issue: men simply want knowledge
of what a woman has to offer beneath her clothes.
Always. And this both of you must understand.

Cauleen Smith, still from *I Want to See My Skirt*

Day at the Beach

ROKIA, AGE SEVENTEEN

In spring, in my mother's parlor
I peer out the bay window
and see the perennials stretching
through the earth toward the sky;
I realize at that moment, 7 A.M. on the clock,
that I must do the same.
I pack a bag: swimming suit, bikini-style,
like in the British magazines; the album
cover from Masekela's *Grrr*
with Funkadelic's *Free Your Mind . . .*
and Your Ass Will Follow
and the Rolling Stones' *Sticky Fingers*,
inside; a towel that won't be missed;
a comb; two mangoes, one for me
and one for Shango. We'll share
my mangoes and my comb;
shea butter for our skin. On the way back
I'll get a ticket from the movie house.
I'll stuff it in the back pocket of my slacks,
casually—half-in, half-out—as an alibi
in clear sight. My parents will believe
they've made a discovery, Silly girl!
Throwing away your money on movies,
and in a way, they'll be telling more truth
than they know: this artifact of a day
discarded in sunlight and secrecy.

Malick Sidibé, *Pique-Nique à la Chaussée*, 1972

Beach Day

SHANGO, ROKIA'S BOYFRIEND

Imagine: freedom found
in a pair of shoes from London,
a hat from Harlem. No one
could imagine how much liberation
folds in the collar of a shirt,
the cut of a suit, or a beat
seeping from a phonograph.
Rokia, topless, looks as innocent
as a little girl. There's nothing illicit
about her body. She's like art, man,
pure and unmarred by guilt. I could look
at her—look at the joy in her eyes, that is—
and never turn away. I'm just a boy playing
in the sun when we're out here in the foam
of the sea, the cushion of the sand . . .
See her footprints? They make wings in the sand.

Shango Prepares for the Dance

Once, I believed I'd be my father. I
used to mimic his style, his gait, and his talk.
Now, Rokia has freed me with a walk
along the beach. And the tailor's
measuring tape defines our world.
I want to dance with her, be the best-dressed
man there. My big concern.
To grow into my own man—stepping out
from my father's shadow!—depends on how
I move and dress. If anyone questions
my motives tomorrow, they'll be sorry.
I don't mean this as a threat, I simply mean
I'll be my best self: a man dancing with Rokia,
as easily as we walk along a beach.

The Tailor

You've come to me and asked for a dream.
Something you've seen in a magazine you now
want me to make into a reality, to sew,
in effect, a new reality for you. You pay me a visit,
but this is really home for you; yet, like a stranger
you ask for a way to fit in. Well, lucky for you, style

is my business. I can make anything I can see; style
is at home wherever you find it. It's more than a dream;
it's a way to speak to the world, like a stranger
making a new friend. Before you were an outsider; now,
with a new suit or dress, it's as if you're revisiting
a familiar place. You tell me what you want, and I'll sew.

Your part in this is easy. Don't think so
hard about clothes; think about you. Style
must be worn more than the fabric itself. Visit
the possibilities in the pages of *Vogue* and dream
into my fingers. Don't hesitate in this life; now
is the time to tell the onlookers to cease being strangers.

Welcome them to you with new clothes. Don't feel strange
about standing out. Just allow me to sew
the world around your bones in the here and the now
and let history fall at your well-heeled feet. A new style
is always welcomed despite how it bangs against dreams
of uniforms and boots in step, the guns visiting

our homes at night. They want us pinned inside, not to visit
the rest of this world. A new cut to an old suit seems strange
to some, but most will come to appreciate your dream
and will come to me in time, at night, and ask me to sew
their lives into lines that speak peace. A new style
walks. As politicians ask us to wait, we demand Now—

for the freedom to express with our bodies. Now,
don't get me wrong. Clothes only protect flesh; a visit
to a tailor is like going to church. Spirit, always in style,
worships through what one wears. How strange
this world would be if we were all in uniform, sad to sew
a garment for someone who wasn't allowed to dream.

Now, go forth in the alluring clothes of the stranger,
and visit others as if a needle and thread sewed
not just a new style into this world but also a new dream.

Woman Ascending a Staircase

It's hard to imagine, in a back-stair
ascent in a setting like this,
I could be overdressed.
Last week, only one skinny boy
asked me to dance, but I'm
dressing for the arms of Shango.
This dress—from the February *Vogue*, 1967—
yes, a few months old, but not by these standards.
This one photo of a woman . . . (What
to say about that which has no need for words?)
The one of her walking across a street, pigeons
scurrying around her high-heeled feet,
men craning their necks and women—
the other women, barely in focus—
passing her by, trying to ignore her
to no avail. When I saw this dress,
I told the tailor, "This one. Just like this."
He looked at me and said, "Child,
do you know the responsibility that comes
with wearing a dress like this?"
I paid him and smiled.
Now, as I climb stairs to a door to this dance,
I want to hear Shango's gaze over the music.

Cauleen Smith, still from *I Want to See My Skirt*

"Masked Man" Visits the Tailor

"My name is Timba, and I need a suit."
The tailor looked at me with the slyest smile
I'd ever seen. "What do you mean by 'suit'?"
he asked. Other customers were in the shop.
He looked at them and then back at me.
I wanted to walk out, but I told him I'd wait.
A full hour passed. I looked through the fabrics.
And the variety of zippers . . .
How many ways can you zip up a pair of pants?
When we talked, it turned out
all I could afford was a custom pair of pants
and a leftover shirt from a customer
who never paid. But then I saw something
I'd only seen in magazines: a ski mask.
My mouth hung open: "How—"
The tailor cut me off, "Don't ask. You
want this, too?" I thought of the mystery
of a masked man. "Yes. I'll take it."
He gave me the shirt for half price.
He measured me for slacks, as he called them.
I walked back to the zippers. "This one,"
I said, holding it up to the light,
"This gold one. For my fly."

Malick Sidibé, *Je Suis le Masque de Fer*

"Masked Man" in the Mirror before the Dance

I won't crawl to him; I'll step,
knowing the risk involved.
I'll take a chance, but if a boy sees my face,
I don't know if I can face his response.
He may not be the kind of boy who'd date
a boy, let alone a boxer. Will my swollen eyelids
and crooked nose reveal where I'm from?
The first round is always danced
on nervous legs. But every fighter needs
a lover; a man can't fight through rage
alone. Sometimes, what's waiting for him
at home gets him through the fight.
Sometimes, the unknown gets the blood
pumping. How else does a man know
what life has to offer, how good is he
if he doesn't meet his fear, toe-to-toe?

The Dance

The tailor has been busy turning bodies into art
for the dance floor. Dancers find their voice in their feet.
Hips and arms command the music to start.
The dance is where the shy make their mark
on those who never knew the beauty of loose limbs.
Yes, the tailor has been busy and bodies are art.
For most, it's just a chance to play their part.
Hats, scarves, shoes: everyone caters to a whim.
Hips and arms command music to start.
No parents. No gossip. Teens exchange clothes à la carte.
A tie becomes a scarf. A shirt, now a dress. Ideas meet.
The tailor has been busy turning bodies into art.
On the floor, everyone looks smart.
No time for judgment while the young keep discreet.
Under the sway of hips and arms, the music starts.
If this is a new day, so much fun can't be work
but a language that gets butts out of seats,
the tailor must be busy; these bodies are art.
They're hipped and armed; let the music start.

Malick Sidibé, *Nuit de Noël (Happy-Club)*

Malick Sidibe, *Couple de danseurs de Beatles—Club Bagadadji*

Malick Sidibé, *Fans de James Brown*, 1965

Cauleen Smith, still from *I Want to See My Skirt*

Snapshots

THE PHOTOGRAPHER'S FIRST VIEW OF THE DANCE AT DOSSALO'S, 1967

Neither kangas nor Kaunda suits appear,
no mud cloth, no pagnes, nothing traditional
here. The first thing I notice is the style
of how the men and women move in these threads.
A new look covers their bodies; it lives in their eyes,
and all I have to do is capture it before anyone gets caught.

TWO WOMEN SIDE-BY-SIDE, IN SHORT DRESSES

I ask them, *How will you look if caught
by your parents in these dresses?* They appear
surprised by the question, but their eyes
don't even meet before they strike a pose. Tradition
is immediately dismissed. Over time, the thread
of history is rewoven as they raise fists, boxing-style.

MAN IN STINGY-BRIM HAT, SUIT JACKET, AND BRIEFCASE

He asks for a prop: a table with flowers? Not his style
but he makes it work. The tie and shirt are caught
in the kinetic pattern of lines and drape, then the threads,
man. He's sharp. A cigarette dangles from his lip, appears
to almost talk for him. In his briefcase, a new tradition
will emerge. Plans for a new cut of suit flash behind his eyes.

MAN IN VEST WITH OPEN ARMS

Pinstripe pants, pinstripe vest, pinpoint eyes.
The mouth doesn't so much smile as open, styled
like his arms, which welcome the crowd in a tradition
he's building from love. Eyes on his vest catch
the embroidery on its border. At first glance, it appears
nothing matches, until his arms open like two woven threads.

WOMAN IN SUNGLASSES AND NEWSBOY CAP

The skirt drapes her legs in stripes. The threads
contrast the oval sunglasses covering her eyes.
But why smile behind shades? The camera appears
to know more than I do. Her open-palm pose, her style.
What she wears offers a fresh take on tradition.
And her black T-shirt and cap bespeak, *I won't get caught.*

COUPLE, BACK-TO-BACK

After all, it's a couple's party. If they get caught,
they're going together. There isn't a thread
between them, swaying into each other, away from tradition.
What is hidden by his sunglasses reveals itself in her eyes.
His bell-bottom slacks and her minidress just adorn their style.
When they walked in, they knew it was an appearance.

ROKIA AND SHANGO DANCE

On the dance floor, tradition is found in their eye
contact. His thread-slim tie, her bare-shouldered dress: style
speaks for them. Everything appears worth it, being caught.

The Next Day

Morning, and the steps of last night followed me home
like the cologne of Shango still on my dress,
wafting through the chiffon, lifting, lifting,
and holding me upright in memory, into a new day.
I see the silhouette of his body, the silhouette he danced
in. Between the music and the dim light and the scent
of him, summer came in one dance. The night spent
quickly, an entire season in one night. Maybe the night
never happened. How many memories hold in focus
without some patina? To think an experience could
breathe like a fantasy, seems a fantasy. Watching
sun pour through my room, the sound of the house
wakens me, rocks over me, over a void my body filled once.

a·dult| əˈdəlt, ˈaˌdəlt | *noun* a person who is fully grown or developed: Teams of teens wore minidresses and suits under their traditional garb, defying disapproval by *adults.* • a fully developed animal. • **Law** a person who has reached the age of majority. • the age when a person is legally considered a full adult, in most contexts 18 or 21: The teens, particularly the girls, gain control of their emotions when restrictions require them to take control of their lives, often well before the age of majority as full *adults.* Too often, they're seen as prey for the male *adult* species. *Adjective* **1.** (of a person or animal) fully grown or developed: With love full bloom in their hearts, were these teens not living an *adult* situation? • **2.** of or for adult people: *adult* desire, *adult* responsibility | all the perils of an *adult* life. • **3.** emotionally and mentally mature: Once out of their parents' home, roaming through the night in clandestine locations, they carried themselves with *adult* aplomb. • **4.** sexually explicit or pornographic (used euphemistically to refer to a movie, book, or magazine). Even as they explored each other's bodies, their hands learning the contours of each other's never-seen-by-another's-eyes parts, their dreams were *adult,* as their actions remained juvenile. *verb* [no object; informal] behave in a way characteristic of a responsible adult, especially by accomplishing mundane but necessary tasks: They *adulted* but with an innocence they won't have to regret in the years ahead. Let's just say *adulting* in this style remains reserved for the youth.

DERIVATIVES adultify *verb*—to treat a child or teenager as an adult • As an older brother, Shango knew he'd show his younger siblings not just how to dress to express cool but also how to live in their skin. He had to *adultify* his relationship to them, so they could enjoy their youth.

WHEN I
WAKED, . . .

Being a Black man in the United States of
America, even up here in Ohio, where they act
like all the racists are down south still, he was
used to cops stopping him for not a thing in
this world.

— MICHAEL PARKER, *All I Have in This World*

"When I Waked, I Cried to Dream Again"

The following are excerpts from a Smithsonian Folklife and Oral History Project transcript of a series of recordings between Miles Jenkins and his uncle Darren Jenkins, Bearer of Tradition for this project. Three recordings were made between May 28, 2018, and September 15, 2018. Darren Jenkins speaks of a scholar whose work was transformative for him as a writer.

INTERVIEW CONDUCTED ON MAY 28, 2018

. . . If I had known her this well in life, I would've understood why she left me in her will, which is still a bit of a mystery to me. What I've come to understand, though, is that she knew me better than I knew myself.

When someone dies and names you in a will, it's kind of a mystery gift: you open the bag and whatever's there is yours, like it or not. And, no matter what people say, that's no way to discover someone loves you—get some money, get a house, get some jewelry . . . none of that stuff matters: what they really leave you is a relationship, you know? Now, keep in mind, Dr. Melba Higginbottom was not a friend of mine, we only met once in life, but sometimes you meet people and even a brief exchange with them can change your fate forever.

First of all, she scared the shit out of me. She was one of those people who you'd want to sit with and ask questions of, but you also didn't wanna look the fool. So, I spoke to her in like haikus and shit. *[Laughter]* You know? Talking to a legend in Shakespearean scholarship like Higginbottom was intimidating, but now, talking to her ghost? Definitely an extreme sport. I can dive into a dusty archive to satisfy my curiosities, but I don't fuck with Ouija boards, so some questions just have to go unanswered.

But any serious reader of Shakespeare—even a hobbyist, like myself—would be pulled in by this final, unpublished work of hers, man. Her real gift was her ability to bring disparate subjects together to show their connections. That's . . . that's what I learned from her. Those connections opened new worlds . . . Finding connections between moments that you had no idea would connect with another. Just to break it down: Higginbottom took the position that since Shakespeare stole from other authors, stole from historical events and current events, why shouldn't she. In her words, "Dude was a master thief." And she loved pop culture—*Real Housewives of Atlanta* to *The Masked Singer*—so Shakespeare was a kinda kindred spirit for her. Shakespeare would've been keeping up with the Kardashians, for sure.

※

Say what? Yeah. You're right, poetry; she did that, too. But her real groove was what we now call critical fabulation. She basically took New Historicism to a whole other level. *[inaudible]* I know, right?! Deep.

Higginbottom focused a lot on people and how they lived, power dynamics and all that. To say that she was a bit obsessed with these concerns would not be hype; I mean, she was like fanatical. Not to talk about the dead and all, but homegirl was a little strange. I'm saying, without her credentials—and, mind you, she was heavy: got her PhD from Cambridge in seventy-seven, a thesis on Shakespeare's Moors—yeah, without that, people would probably just see her as some freak. But Higginbottom, eccentricities and all, was above all else a first-rate Shakespeareanist, which would be impressive enough, but growing up in Cleveland's Hough housing projects in the sixties? I mean, she was there during the uprising as a teenager.

※

Yeah, yeah . . . Always reppin CLE. Like us, she was educated but she came up in the streets. Code switching, nephew. You gotta stay nimble. Keep moving forward with an eye on where you came from, which is a lesson I got from her. When I got my PhD, I never wanted to get to a point where I couldn't talk to folks I grew up with. In that same spirit, she managed to carve out a life staying in the Cleveland area, teaching at Cleveland State and all that. And being a woman of excess in every area of her life, she built a home there: a timber-framed "wattle-and-daub." Although the style of the home was more façade than function—the interior had radiant bathroom floors, a screening room, and a crystal grotto—her homeowners' association was all fucked up over it. But Higginbottom just paid the fine and kept building, like the

G that she was, and, in fact, the more they talked shit, the more square footage she added, until she reached just over three thousand square feet. The sista was smooth and tough, a pianist's hand in a Kevlar glove. Well, finally, the HOA gave in, and dispensation was granted when she agreed to install a concrete fence, blocking the view of the house from the street. It was some ugly shit, man, but she got the W.

*

This was classic Higginbottom. You see, this sista's persistence in all pursuits became so legendary that her surname engendered a verb form, Higginbottom, or Higginbottomed, in the past tense; or, in the infinitive, *to Higginbottom the situation*, as when someone manages to accomplish something through preternatural persistence. Once when a Higginbottom acolyte used the verb form in an MLA committee meeting, the committee chair, a linguist of international renown, dismissed it as another form of *to Bartleby a situation*, to which the acolyte clarified with some authority that *to Bartleby is to do nothing; to Higginbottom is to do everything in one's power.* After fifteen minutes of this digression from the meeting, trying to define the verb with metaphors ranging from Eugene V. Debs to sit-down protests to suicide bombings, the chair acquiesced to the acolyte. Yeah, the chair was, in effect, Higginbottomed.

So, when she died, her house was donated to the city of Berea. It's now the site of their historical museum—advertised on the website of the Chamber of Commerce and everything. You could never predict what she would do: Her neighbors were surprised, at the public reading of her will, to find that the house was bequeathed to their shitty little hamlet. The executor of the will, Agnes Muncie, said that she hadn't seen a will in language like this before. I've never heard the reading of a will before myself, so I had no expectations of what one should sound like, but I knew it would be dope because Higginbottom wrote it, but, still, I wasn't ready.

※

. . . Trust me: I was sitting there asking the same question. Why was *I* there? Like I said, I didn't know her that well; we weren't what you would call friends. We first met in Washington, DC, over drinks at a bar during a conference, in ninety-six. See, I walk into the conference bar, and take the only seat available, which is next to her. I'm reading a book on Black screenwriters, right? And she surprises me because she knows some of their names; everyone knows the directors, but few people know the screenwriters. So, we start talking about the structure of *Killer of Sheep* and how, in each vignette, there's a little joy. And I say to her:

"I'm so tired of people telling me about the beauty of poverty in that film." She looks out facing the bottles behind the bar, like she's picturing the scenes in her head. "Everyone wants to talk about the high art in the struggles of Black folk. But the shit is just a struggle."

Then she turns to look at me, and I take in her intense gaze: "Every scene turns on an act of love, and that's really the plot of that film," she says. I had to hold on that for a moment. I'm thinking, *Yeah . . . I can see that.* So I say:

"Yeah, I see it."

"The girl with the dog mask."

"Yes! I love that kid."

"That's what that's about," she says, pointing a finger at me. "A child playing. That says all you need to know. Somewhere in that child's life there's love."

She pauses and turns to stare out again. I just sit with her for a few, in a kind of silence. Surrounding us, just the din of bar life, which is just as empty as no sound. And I'm sitting there, and I know she'll say something else when she wants.

And then she hits me with it.

" 'No tongue! All eyes! Be silent!' this is what the world says to the Black man." She says this like she expects me to do some call and response and shit, but I have nothing.

"Act four, scene one, *The Tempest*," she says. "Prospero says this shit to Ariel. Basically, do as I say. No backtalk. You see what I tell you to see."

"I've heard that my whole life," I say, which is all I have to contribute.

"I know you have," she says, "I know you have."

✳

No? You haven't seen *Killer of Sheep*? Black neorealism. A must see, nephew. That early scene in it stood out to both of us. There's this little girl who walks around in a rubber mask, a mask of a hound dog. Her parents fight, her father works at a slaughterhouse during the day, and neither of her parents show much evidence of joy in their lives. In the mask, the girl's superpower, despite how sad the dog's face looks, is her ability to play, to retain her innocence, despite what, on the surface, seems like little joy around her in the adult world. I felt all this watching it, but I couldn't quite put into words what I felt until that conversation. Now I see these moments of joy in every scene of the film, and there are days when I feel like that little girl when I want to hold on to some joy despite what's happening around me.

We never spoke at length again.

✳

[Darren stares off for a beat. Miles nudges him.]

My bad . . . so, the best way to explain why I was in her will is like I said before. Sometimes you just connect deeply with someone even though you don't have much history with them, but the little history you have means something—could be good, could be bad, but a brief encounter can change your fate. That conversation was mine . . . We were just friendly enough to wave at each other, even once blowing kisses to each other while riding opposing escalators at a later conference, so I was surprised to get the notice that I was included in her will and then surprised at the reading of her will to find she left her unfinished manuscript, "When I Waked, I Cried to Dream Again," to me. The best answer I have is that I don't know why she chose me, and her will didn't help any, either.

Here, I brought it with me. *[The unfolding of paper]* The language in her will . . . it read crazy, man. I'm gonna stumble through this, so excuse me:

Item Six, I, Melba Higginbottom, bequeath unto the belabored scholar Darren Jenkins the manuscript and the capsule in the handeth of the town execut'r of this will Agnes Muncie, jointress unto Mr. John Q. Muncie. The manuscript wilt beest edited and did complete within six months or 'twill beest did destroy according to the true meaning of this, mine wilt.

Nephew, when she read that shit out loud, I didn't understand a word. Just my name. But the executor held up a thumb drive and the hard-copy manuscript and motioned in my direction. I looked behind me to realize she was speaking to me, so I stood up and took the handwritten, ink-smudged pages.

[Sound of the pages in Darren's hands.]

And now I have less than six months to make these edits and present it to a publisher; otherwise, it'll be destroyed.

❄

[Darren sighs. Silence. Fifteen-second pause on the tape.]

Ah, I know. I see you smiling . . . I didn't answer your question about my youth. Well, nephew, nothing I read influenced me in my youth. I wasn't the reader then that I am today, just comic books. But an incident that involved your uncle Gerald and me . . . and your grandmother. This stayed with me. You see your Grammy now with Alzheimer's, but her common-sense quotient was genius level when I was a kid, and she took no shit off no body. It must've been 1973; I was eight years old; your uncle Gerald, fifteen. It's fall, so we're wearing overcoats, but we just left church, so we also have on suits underneath. Mom brings us to this plaza where she has to see this lady, a seamstress. Gerald and I are just kids, so we're bored as hell. We ask if we could go to the drugstore at the end of the plaza to get some candy. We walk down to People's Drug, and once we get in there, well, of course, I have to look at the comic books, which your uncle Gerald has no interest in. You know, of my brothers, I'm the nerd. So Gerald goes to pay, and when he finishes, he tells me to come on.

We begin our walk back to the other end of this plaza, which was just a block long. Well, we get about halfway there, and these cops pull up, and I mean they come in hot, gangsta their squad car right up on the sidewalk. We're standing there with our mouths open like *what the fuck*. But we're young and don't know shit, so we think we're about to watch them apprehend some bad guys, like on TV; they jump out of the car with their guns drawn. Still, we're thinking, this is some cool shit we're about to witness. In our minds, finally, the day is getting exciting.

Next thing you know, they're standing in front of us, guns in our faces, yelling for us to drop the bag of candy and to get against the wall. Gerald elbows me to act like him and raise my hands; I was clutching the inside of my pockets like I could pull myself down in there and hide. I finally reach for the sun. I'd seen enough westerns to know that when a gun is pulled on you, you raise your hands, but that shit doesn't come naturally. The most natural thing to do is to freeze. You don't want to move anything; you want time to stop, but it doesn't work like that. That's why some people pee on themselves or even take a shit, frozen in fear. Well, a few seconds later, another car of cops pulls up, also like they're about to nab bank robbers or some shit. At this point, I start crying, which pisses Gerald off, because he's already mad and looking at the cops like if they didn't have guns, he'd have their asses.

Well, just when I think this shit can't get worse, Mom comes flying out of the seamstress shop. Man, she starts cussing these cops out like they stole something. They tell her to calm down, which makes her cuss even more. Then she tells them to explain what the fuck was going on that they felt the need to pull guns on her children. These Keystone muthafuckas look at one another, until the one cop, the one who jumped out of the car first, says, "We had a report of two individuals, fitting your sons' descriptions . . . shoplifting."

"Shoplifting?!" she says, and then she looks at us like, *were you?* And we just shake our heads like, *hell no.*

Man, I don't remember what happened next, but we walked away, with Mom still cussing them out as we walked back to her car.

❋

. . . Yeah . . . "Damn" is right. So, to your question, the manuscript gets into these kinda moments, the moments we carry with us, but we have to tamp them down, walking around in the company of white people like everything is fine in the world. Higginbottom looks at a situation like that, and she ties it to Shakespeare. She always mentioned, pretty much in every talk she gave, that if Shakespeare were alive today, he'd be writing about the relationship between Black people and the police.

She made no apologies for being seen as an angry Black woman or uppity, and she never tried to soften her stance on anything for mixed company. She was always herself.

If you can imagine this, at a dry-ass cocktail party once, the party's host—another Shakespeareanist, whose name I won't say here because he's a colleague—makes a performance of his magnanimity by inviting Higginbottom into a conversation about Shakespearean actors. This after going on and on about how Olivier was the natural heir to this dude named Burbage, he asked her, "What do you think?" To which Higginbottom, in classic Higginbottom fashion, asked, "What was the longest running Shakespeare play on Broadway?" She knew the answer, but she wanted this scholar, who put Olivier up on a white-men-only pedestal, to say it.

"Oh . . . that's a good question."

"The quality of my question is not in question."

"Well, of course not, I just meant—"

"—*Othello*. Paul Robeson's *Othello*. And he proved it could be done without Blackface for two hundred and ninety-six performances in 1943 and 1944, so why Olivier felt the need to Black it up twenty years later, I'll never know."

She hit him with the highbrow lowbrow. She would never have to ask, directly, why don't you include James Earl Jones or Earle Hyman or, yeah, Robeson. (And you went to Howard, theater major, so I don't even have to tell you about Ira Aldridge.) She simply, with dignity, refused to play into the mythology.

But that was one of the last times people saw her in public. She had become a recluse in her house, not a hoarder or anything, but a recluse. People mentioned at the funeral that they often saw her sitting by a window, working at her desk. She had retired at sixty-two, and no one had seen her in years. Her colleagues would invite her to dinner parties and events in the department—she had emeritus status—but the invitations went unanswered.

[Tape clicks off.]

＊

INTERVIEW CONDUCTED ON JULY 16, 2018

After Darren Jenkins has spent two months with the manuscript, Miles Jenkins checks in with his uncle. With many asides in this portion of the interview, the archivists decided, after much debate, to include the tangents, uncut.

MJ: So, how's it going with the deadline? You look . . . you look a little tired.

DJ: I know I don't look good. Yeah, I'm tired. To say that the manuscript haunts me would be an understatement. It's like a specter, willing me to action from the afterlife. A few weeks ago, in the middle of the night, I felt my bed move, man, serious business. Shit woke me up; it was four forty A.M. I had been dreaming of my childhood. The west side of Akron. My teenage years, a house party, a black lightbulb, and my glow-in-the-dark teeth smiling beneath it, as I prayed for a slow song. The strange part wasn't the dream but the fact that I knew I was dreaming. I mean, who knows they're in a dream while inside the dream itself? But let me tell you: I felt the comfort of that space, that house party; that light blacker than our bodies, making our bodies glow; the music those young bodies made—all of it frivolous and all of it necessary, all at once.

"Throw your hands in the air,
And wave 'em like you jus' don't care!"

And every night I dreamed, and every night I went back to that party, getting closer to a slow song, and every morning I woke before dawn, before I could get my slow dance on under the vibrato of Luther Vandross' voice.

I kept thinking about the LED digits on my clock . . . wondering why at this hour. Then, I gave up. I couldn't sleep, padding my way to my desk after making a pot of coffee, I pulled out the manuscript, and I saw Higginbottom's phone number in the lower left corner of the title page, area code 440.

I tried to ignore it, but that shit started sinking in, man. I would lie in bed, tossing and turning, intermittently looking at the clock: twelve oh five A.M., two twelve A.M., four forty A.M. and then time to get up, go through the manuscript, and start my day on campus. Since I couldn't think of anything other than the political morass of the country, the declining health of my mother, and Higginbottom's manuscript, I opted for the latter to distract me from the pain of the two former. I mean, what could I do? I held the yellowed, dog-eared pages in my hands, flipped through them, and came to understand Higginbottom more through her commitment to this off-beat project of personal letters, a mysterious thumb drive that only had some music on it, just the one song; news clippings; poems in staggered lines; historical asides; poems set in squares within squares; and poems, all of them, cast in the voices of characters from *The Tempest* and in the voices of contemporary figures in conversation with those characters. Why would her last project be a collection of poems that resembled the remnants from a Dos Passos novel? Greater yet, why entrust it to me?

So, daily, at my four forty A.M. alarm, I settle into my armchair, and I transport to this imaginary island—the Devil Strip, she named it—with Black inhabitants, and the storm of Higginbottom's pages carries me into her world. And I do mean *pages*: The first surprise was that the thumb drive didn't have files on it, man. It only had two MP3 sound files. One file had a full version of James Brown's "Get Up, Get into It, Get Involved," and the other had the same song but all instrumental. *[James Brown's voice bleeds in and then the horns kick in.]* When I listen to the music, it becomes a kind of soundtrack to my reading, but I can only listen to the instrumental version. The lyrics sing like ghosts in my head.

MJ: Can you read a little bit of it? Now I'm curious.

DJ: I can read from this intro section. It's full of tangents, which I love, but hold on, youngin; she does go there.

❊

[Darren Jenkins reads from the original, handwritten manuscript.]

After a long rumination, I now return to the page, exactly one year to this Martin Luther King Jr. Day holiday, during which time I've studied the case of Tamir Rice, twelve years old, slain by rookie police officer Tim Loehmann. I'm trying to hold my pen like a gun, a gun held sideways like young gangstas hold guns in films. I'm trying to inhabit the skin of the Black man in Loehmann's imagination—not Tamir Rice. The Black man in Loehmann's imagination couldn't be farther

from Tamir Rice or any of the Black men I've known
and those I've loved and those I've made love to and
those in whose eyes I could see God. I'm writing in the
vein of the imaginary monster in the mind of Prospero,
the imaginary monster he wants all of us to see as a true
monster, Caliban, who, like Tamir, gets explained to us
without his beauty. If you destroy something of beauty,
you have to find an excuse for your ~~crime~~ actions. O'
how white cops fill their dreams with ~~niggers~~ Black men!

[Inaudible language from Jenkins.]
[Papers fall to the floor.]

MJ: Not what I expected.

DJ: It's full of surprises. This is just the beginning of a five-thousand-word intro to the manuscript. Did I mention that this was handwritten? *[We hear Jenkins pick up the pages.]* I realized that Higginbottom wanted me not only to edit these pages but also to get them typed into a Word.doc. I should've been insulted—I mean, typing?—but I felt a need to answer the call. Something, finally, stirred within me after I read that opening paragraph. And it did ignite something in me, some élan vital, to trace her words in this way. You see, a kind of nihilism had taken root in me over the years, after seeing one killing after another of unarmed Black men on the news. It should've had the opposite effect, but I felt kind of anesthetized. I mean, how else do you get up and go to work in the morning, except to tamp it down and keep it moving? I can't say, *Oh, that news about that brotha who got shot by the police was triggering to me. I can't get in my car and come in to work today.* I mean I should've been saying that shit, I should've been *able* to say that shit, but I'm embarrassed to admit that the killings were becoming a white noise, a cliché, playing in the background. It was all the same story, read on the nightly news like some Gothic lullaby, and I had become a somnambulist of sorts.

Guilt grew over time as I read through Higginbottom's pages. Why hadn't I picked up a pen, like a gun—or a gun like a pen!—and fought back yet? I had to think about that one for a while, not really having a good answer.

❋

D. L. Hughley, the comedian, once said that the most dangerous place for a Black man to live is in a white man's imagination. I made a meal out of that, mulling over the words. I realized how it's also dangerous for a Black man to visit the white imagination, to get comfortable there, and to move in. Hughley's words tapped into a fear of mine: I feel as if I've been turning, becoming more accommodating, speaking out less. It's like, year after year, I can feel the bass draining from my voice.

[A pause. Inaudible mumbling.]

MJ: Where'd you just go?

DJ: I'm here . . . I'm good.

[Another pause. Jenkins collects himself, wiping his eyes.]

MJ: O-kay, so, shifting gears, why did Higginbottom get so obsessed with this project?

DJ: Tamir Rice. When you read her take on it, her words just . . . man, it just takes you over.

[Jenkins reads further into the handwritten manuscript.]

THE SHOOTING OF TAMIR RICE ON VIDEO

He shuffled his feet and the camera caught him bored on November 22, 2014; few people saw him trying to have fun. The grass at Cudell Recreation Center was covered in patches of snow, and Tamir wanted to play like it was summer. It was work to play like a boy, and no girls came around to give him reason to act like a man. Cleveland boys wore suits or hoodies, carried guns or books—depending on the day of the week, depending on who was watching. Tamir played in the park outside the rec center, where everything fell silent, no balls bounced in the snow. Girls stayed inside from the cold, keeping their skin warm by the radiators. No cameras in their homes. The cameras trained on boys in the park. Tamir looked bored, I'm telling you, bored and cold. He made snowballs and threw them into the ether. People walked by, but he played on. Sometimes he pulled out an Airsoft, pointing it, Bang! Bang! at people, who walked away, not ran, seeing that Tamir was just trying to have some fun. Plastic pellets never fired.

The surveillance video can't capture details of his face. Cleveland police try pushing in for a close-up, try to explain what happened, but Tamir just blurs even more.

Where is the child with the toy gun? The twelve-year-old boy? The police said they thought he was twenty. Huh?

Remember that episode of The Andy Griffith Show, *"Runaway Kid," when Opie plays cowboy with his friends, all carrying six-shooters that look like real guns, pearl handles and all? The sheriff—his pa, Andy—pulls up, gets out of the police cruiser, and Opie and his friends tell the sheriff, "Draw!" But Andy doesn't—the sheriff of Mayberry never carries a gun—so Opie shoots, like Tamir does, with his mouth, "Bang! Bang!" Andy reels back, grabs his heart, pretending he's been mortally wounded.*

Tamir died on November 23, the next day, the day after he was playing in the park, after he was shot playing in the park. The day before, when the police showed up, Tamir was sitting with his head down on a picnic table in the gazebo. Bored to death. The police cruiser barrels through the park on grass, right up to the gazebo. They come in so fast, Tamir jumps up and starts walking to see what's happening. On video we see the police cruiser pull up, and before the car settles to a stop, we see Tamir fall. The officers get out of the car; the officer on the passenger side, closest to Tamir, was close enough to shoot from his seat. Tamir is shot in his torso, as officers train to do, in less than two seconds.

How many hours tick away in two seconds
and whose watch keeps time?

Yes, other kids were in the park, and they fell back as soon as the police pulled across the grass to the gazebo. Soon, Tamir's fourteen-year-old sister comes running over. An officer tackles her. She's screaming, but the camera has no audio; it's an empty scream. They keep her restrained, despite her void screams and lack of weapon, until backup comes.

When Tamir lived, he played in his school's drumline, and he enjoyed basketball. Two activities that keep a boy's hands busy, not pulling on his waistband, as the police reported. The "pulling on his waistband" presents a defense for the police, justifies the shooting. A twelve-year-old Black boy with his hands not handling a basketball or drumming with sticks presents reasonable cause. "Show me your hands, show me your hands, show me your hands!" One officer reports he said this, but he was driving the car, and the car hadn't rested to a stop when Tamir fell. It takes nearly four seconds to say "show me your hands" three times fast. The driver, not the shooter, gets out of the car, gun drawn, and stands near the front of the cruiser with his gun trained on Tamir,

who is writhing on the ground, out of sight from the camera,
occluded by the car. The shooter takes cover behind the trunk
of the car, peeking over, looking down at Tamir's body.

Whose shadow casts farther,
the standing cop, smoke rising from his gun,
or the shot boy, sprawled on the ground?

In the "Runaway Kid" episode, later, Opie and his two
gun-slinging friends decide that they'll play a trick on the
sheriff, Andy. They decide to release the brake on Andy's
parked police cruiser and push it in front of a "fireplug."
The deputy, Barney Fife, comes along, sees Andy's cruiser
in front of the hydrant, and, you know, the law's the law,
so he writes Andy a ticket. Andy pleads his case to his
deputy, telling him that he's never in five years as sheriff
ever parked his car in front of a fireplug, and Barney, see-
ing his point, lets Andy go free. It's comedy, so the action
moves fast, even in Mayberry. Soon, Andy goes outside to
move his cruiser, setting a good example for the citizens
of Mayberry, and along comes Opie, still dangling two
pistols from his waistband. Opie tells his pa that he and
his friends moved his car:

[audio of The Andy Griffith Show *kicks in]*

ANDY
I still can't see how my car got in front of that fireplug.

OPIE

I know how, Pa.

ANDY

You do?

OPIE

Yeah, Steve and Tommy and me pushed it there . . .
You gonna arrest 'em? I think you could get a confession
out of 'em.

ANDY

Well, uh, why shouldn't I arrest you, too?

OPIE

I didn't push very hard.

[laugh track]

ANDY

Oh, I see, that does make a difference.
[laugh track]
Well, uh, how come they pushed my car in front of the
fireplug?

OPIE

Oh, just for a joke, Pa.

[Inaudible mumbling. Rustling of paper in Darren's hands. Long pause.]

MJ: Hmm . . . That show was so long ago.

DJ: Not really.

[Tape ends.]

❋

[Two months later. September 15, 2018. The uncle and nephew meet again to finish the interview.]

MJ: You look . . . Where are you with the manuscript now?

DJ: I finished it.

MJ: You're finished? On that deadline? I didn't . . . that was fast.

DJ: I felt the pressure, but I settled into a groove. My alarm stopped going off at four forty A.M.; I would already be awake. I might hear an inner voice telling me to sit at the desk, but I didn't need coaxing. Little else held my attention. The trees kept losing leaves, and I couldn't be bothered to rake them. Children would kick through them on their way back and forth to school, and I tried to remember when I was that young. Watching these kids with their lives ahead of them, finding a way to play even while so much was dying around them . . .

I would read passages of "When I Waked, I Cried to Dream Again" aloud to myself, and it became a soundtrack as much as James Brown's piercing demands, which started to fade in intensity the more I listened. The only music was Higginbottom's verse:

A *mother wails for a dying son,*
like a son's last breath
cries out for his mother.

I would approach my desk by approaching the challenge within: If I hoped to live not simply day to day, aimlessly, but to truly open my mouth with an urgent plea, to speak urgency into others, I first had to honor someone who lived her life as I wished to live. I see the manuscript, the fragments of a mother explaining to the world that her child is not a monster, just a boy at play.

Tamir was outrunning the imagined Tamir, dodging in and out of boyhood, morphing between the twenty-year-old Caliban captured on video and a twelve-year-old child with a toy. He skipped through the imaginations of rookie police, the pixels masking him on video. And, so, I typed . . . I got into it, man; I typed away and the words came rushing after him and after the next boy, one after the other.

IRA ALDRIDGE WAS HERE

Coal-black is better than another hue.

—AARON, IN *Titus Andronicus*,
BY WILLIAM SHAKESPEARE, ACT 4, SCENE 2

fair[1] | fer | *adjective* **1.** in accordance with the rules or standards; legitimate: We used a *fair*, impartial process, selecting the most qualified for the job. • just or appropriate in the circumstances: *To be fair,* yes, this young man running through my neighborhood presents a problem. • *archaic* (of a means or procedure) gentle; not violent: The taser is a *fair* means to subdue a suspect. • *Baseball* (of a batted ball) within the field of play marked by the first and third baselines. • *Baseball* pertaining to the fair part of the field: Robinson, number 42, hit the ball into *fair* territory, but the umpire said it was out. **2.** (of hair or complexion) light; blond: The sista died her hair a *fair* hue, but her skin . . . • (of a person) having a light complexion or blond hair: Light. Bright. She's so *fair* she could damn near pass for white. **3.** considerable though not outstanding in size or amount: He interned, he graduated, he paid his dues, but, still, he only had a *fair* bit of a chance. • moderately good though not outstandingly so: He worked through the night, and so he finished ahead of the field, believing maybe now he'd have a *fair* chance of success. **4.** (of weather) fine and dry: Over the field, she bent for hours without fatigue; it was a *fair* September day. **5.** (*archaic, but still used subliminally*) meaning beautiful, attractive: No one spoke of her as a beauty, though she worked in the master's house, but when she got pregnant, her daughter, born with blue eyes, was seen as the *fairest* of all.

Such Sweet Thunder

*Stratford Shakespearean Festival, Duke Ellington and
Billy Strayhorn, 1957*

Minor chords ring across Stratford farmland. We jazz
wherever we're called. Local ears lift to see jazz.

Their hearts hear in places their minds roam.
Oh, if the bard could be Black! She'd be jazz.

If the hogs across the way, just for a moment, were swans
released in a lake, they'd think, *this is the sea*: jazz!

Tell me, if Cleo walked in here right now,
would her stride, royal to her jeweled toes, be jazz?

Britt Woodman's "Hank Cinq" and all them
octave jumps! Slide your trombone, man! Free Jazz!

Now, wipe the sleep from your eyes. The time has come:
Your ideas must speak the language that be jazz.

Who said no Blacks allowed in orchestra seats?
Leave the balcony empty tonight; let that be jazz.

Emmett Till's body found floating in the Tallahatchie River.
Emmett Till's name still rises and, believe me, that be jazz.

Schools in Topeka, Kansas, threw open their doors.
Integration? Call it what you want, but that be jazz.

Tamora's baby came out Black, you say? Damn. The more
I hear about Aaron the Moor, I think. Don't *that* be jazz?

A note above ~ A note below ~ The note between ~
The tonic ~ Enclosed ~ Pivoted up ~ Octave ~ That be jazz.

Oh, if the bard could be Black! Her stride would be royal.
Your ideas must speak. Till's name still rises! That be jazz.

The circle of fourths comes full circle now. Bards:
Duke, Billy! Aaron dances! Enough: Let that be jazz.

Othello the Moor

Only a Black face throwing light could cast shadows.
Only a Black man in charge could garner so many foes.

When only a Black general, when only a Black lover,
when your only Black friend is only yourself . . .

when your Desdemona's so white she doesn't understand
what went wrong. When you're the only Moor, white men

say, "Were I the Moor, I would not be Iago."
Desdemona looks for you with a candle in the daytime,

but you still don't see her. You can't see her
when you can't see yourself. Only the whites

of the eyes of the whites see behind you.
Only the eyes of the Moor eyes the shifting of the day.

When proof appears, who appears behind the man?
Even a handkerchief, dyed in mummy, the color

of your own hand, reveals a foreign touch.
You want to touch the truth with your eyes,

so you can see the magic in the web of your wife.
But even your body, begrimed in beauty, can't be trusted,

if you don't trust your own life.

Aaron the Moor

Believe me, Queen, your swart Cimmerian
Doth make your honor of his body's hue,
Spotted, detested, and abominable.

—BASSIANUS, IN *Titus Andronicus*, BY WILLIAM SHAKESPEARE,
ACT 2, SCENE 3

When we bring others into our lives,
we bring all their life into ours: not only
their family, their secrets, their dirty socks,

but also the warmth of their body next to ours,
which allows us to accept all the challenges
of our lust to belong. Aaron understands,

embracing the blood beating
between him and Tamora and the blood
hammering in his head between him and his foes.

But what's the deal with this brother?
Jumping in bed with a Goth girl like that.
Running around in a country not his own,

beating his chest like that. He acts
like he doesn't know those Andronicus boys
would kill him just as soon as swat a fly.

Aaron, who walks through their starlit lives
like a Black hole filled with every desire
they ever desired, knows the snares of life

and, so, chooses to live his life with a vengeance.
There's power in not apologizing for being
in the world, for embracing the legacy revealed

through, and adorned with, your skin. Yes,
coal-black is better than another hue.
When every doorway opens to another closed door,

why should he behave like a welcomed guest?
His body's hue holds many colors,
and with the gift of his tone, he speaks

his mind through a prism of words. Yeah,
for this alone he could do prison time.
Next thing you know, every crime committed,

even crimes committed by their own hand,
gets blamed on the new brother in town,
and they'd just as soon chop off their own hand

before admitting their own wrong; they'd
cut out a tongue, before allowing someone
to tell the truth, but let's be real:

These people can't be trusted
because they can't trust themselves.
But Aaron knows he's not a traveler

in a foreign land but himself wherever he lands.
*For all the water in the ocean
can never turn the swan's black legs to white.*

The Andronicus may try to narrow
his choice between being a villain or a slave,
as the executioner's blade raises,

but Aaron the Moor, the man, chooses
to lift his truth above the blade,
which can't swing true enough

to silence the cut of his tongue.

A RESOLUTION

Proposing an amendment to the Constitution of the United Stat

Resolved by the Senate and House of Representatives of the United States of America in Congress assembled,

grand·fa·ther. *noun* **1.** the father of one's father or mother: As in, My father's father, my *grandfather,* sharecropped on a farm in Midway, Alabama. Angry all the time, he fled to Ohio for cleaner work, but the same dirt beat him down through his day. **2.** the person who founded or originated something: In 1832, Thomas D. Rice, *grandfather* of Jim Crow, popularizes the phrase with a song of same name, dancing and singing in Blackface, to play a trickster figure, without the wisdom of Anansi, but "nah, uh-uh, nah nah-nahnahnahnahnahnahnah," was all Black people heard when he sang his song.

✳

President of the Senate pro tempore.

Clerk of House of Representatives.

Secy of Senate U.S.

A RESOLUTION

Proposing an amendment to the Constitution of the United

grand·fa·ther. *verb* [with object] **1.** North American informal, exempt (someone or something) from a new law or regulation: Landowners who stole land from indigenous people before the Federal Land Policy and Management Act struck this behavior down in 1976 have been *grandfathered* in to keep these hallowed grounds. *Grandfathered* in, their children's children also can keep the land. Those from whom land was stolen, those who were raided, raped, and run out of town—Greenwood, Oklahoma; Eatonville, Florida; Wilmington, North Carolina; Vicksburg, Mississippi; etc.— leaving their homes behind, have been *grandfathered* in to continue looking for a place to feel safe to call home. **2.** to permit to continue under a grandfather clause: As in, to pass down privilege, which is *grandfathered i*n the blood of law, passed down, *grandfathered* in speech to mean passed down to continue but not to offend just to understand, with your grandfather and with mine, passed from one kin to another, no fault of mine, just passed past your grandfather to mine to me, just law, just an idiom of life, you understand; we all started the same and no *grandfathering* of my grandfather bears down on you, maybe just on your grandfather, son.

How to Celebrate a Revolution

Say something benign about the weather,
to begin, whether it's raining or not,
just exclaim, What a lovely day it is!

using the same inflection with your enemies
as with your neighbors.
Once the sea change comes, people

will prove too bored with disbelief
to argue—surrendering to hope.
At this late hour, when the country believes

it's grown, when twilight teaches
the heartland a lesson about nuance,
we come together to talk

about the news we love to watch,
so we watch another child die muted
on dashcam video; we can almost see

life rise from the child's body
like a silent prayer, floating off
to who knows where.

At this late hour, we nearly give up
on one another: We stay home,
we stop making love, we turn

station after station, looking
for the revolution, believing it
will appear on the higher stations in HD.

*

And why, I ask my aging bones, *why
don't you dance?* Struck dumb, I point
to the TV reminding me, daily,

when the music stopped.

*

At this late hour, the reality show
shows our own lives,
and yet we continue to watch,

hoping, still, for life to work out
but not without some drama.
The screen flickers in the dark.

You turn to your beloved, asking,
Did you understand the ending?

*

You stare hard into each other.

*

You go to bed.

*

My people, if you haven't figured it out yet,
I'm talking about how difficult love is
when a country gets involved,

interrupting those mornings when
a mother waves goodbye to her child,
who, framed in the window of a school bus,

waves back. Mother and child both believing
the other will be okay, but both waving gently
behind glass, fearing the other will break.

Later that night, talking about their day,
they listen to each other so closely
they're almost a better world.

When we look out across the city,
into the faces of others, we're
supposed to believe the world was made

big to keep us from feeling lonely.
When we look out across rural vistas,
we're supposed to believe

the world was made vast
so we could run
as far as we wanted

and no one would tell us to stop.
My dear people, my neighbors,
my conveyors of hopes and workers

of Gordian knots and breakers of stout chains,
I sow within you like a farmer
who plants faith in the harvest,

while the ashes remind us and the births
encourage us and the indolent lounge
under a flaming sky, while the news

carries our fear even as we live it, while
you leave your homes, even today,
to compose love letters and petitions

of yourself in the world, I am staggered
by many acts of hope and the steps taken,
one foot after another, released in this moment

of history carried within you, like a day carries
within it morning and night. Long after today,
we will see a flicker in the mind,

a Polaroid of memory shaken into focus.
Imagine, before the show of your life fills
with static snow on screen, you look outside

and decide—not see but *decide*—there is snow
on the front lawn; you jump
on the white dance floor,

stomping with your boots until
your neighbors come outside to see
just what the hell is going on. Well,

infected by your groove, they unplug, they
join in; we all do, and we continue long into the night,
into the coming day, a Soul Train of revolt

lining rural routes, and filling streets
in our cities with our dance.

Notes

"Hex": I think of this poem as a response to the last line of Amiri Baraka's "Ka'Ba"—"What will be/ the sacred word?"—and in conversation with Lynda Hull's "Spell for the Manufacture & Use of a Magic Carpet." I don't know how anyone writes a poem without the inspiration of poems that came before. I'm constantly calling on our ancestors.

"asterisk": I developed the definition poem in my second book, *M-A-C-N-O-L-I-A*, but I haven't used it in another book since. In *M-A-C-N-O-L-I-A*, I created it to show the turning of the mind of a precocious child, a child who not only spent time with a dictionary but who also needed to cast a *spell* over her life to survive. In this case, I thought it was worth bringing this nonce form back into play to wrap my mind around the language that's hard to articulate when we talk about fraught subjects, what's kept out of the record, the many asterisks that represent the lacunae in cases of discrimination.

The Tempest and "Tamir Rice Case" sequence: One of the biggest surprises I've experienced in middle age is my involuntary desire to protect young people. I've read that the brain's chemistry shifts in your forties, and empathy gets an upgrade. There's other research to the contrary, though, that shows that many people harden in their tendency to believe in stereotypes, which amplifies their impulse for othering. For myself, at least, I know here in my fifties, I'm surprised at what brings tears to my eyes for others, whether witnessing their joy or their pain. So, when I hear reports of adults in uniform justifying why they felt the need to shoot a child on sight, in less than two seconds, I'm clear that this person is not psychologically equipped to carry a weapon.

From where does an idea like *a Black body presents a threat* emerge? When did the Western world begin thinking of the Black body both as undesirable and as a hypersexualized object; as both necessary for slave labor and yet lazy; or as a threat and, all at once, as a joke? Wondering about these origins has not risen to the nomenclature of cliché. No, sadly, we don't ask these questions enough.

I've been thinking about this topic since I was a child standing with a white adult pointing a gun in my face, and the many cliché encounters that followed throughout my life. We—Black people—are taught that the best strategy to survive these stinging moments of life-threatening racism is to stay calm, but I want to know what was the fillip that lit this insidious flame.

I'm not alone in my inquiry. Early Modernist scholars, particularly African American Shakespearean scholars, have been going in on this topic for a minute now. In *The Cambridge Companion to Shakespeare and Race*, Patricia Akhimie locates the seriousness in racist humor in the early modern period in her chapter "Racist Humor and Shakespearean Comedy." One moment stands out in bold relief to me, when she points out that Shakespearean racist humor ". . . reveals the production and maintenance of groups, processes of inclusion and exclusion, and of hierarchization. These are the building blocks of racism." And building on this point, she goes on, in "A Whole Theater of Others," an episode of the Folger Shakespeare Library's *Shakespeare Unlimited* podcast, to say, "How are stereotypes created and how are they maintained? One of the ways is through communal laughter"—which is to say, those in on the joke laugh at those who are othered. Over time, something as seemingly simple as ridicule devolves into justifying violence against the ridiculed.

"A Tempest": This poem is in response to Aimé Césaire's play by the same name and the many tempests we feel in our lives, particularly the microaggressions that wear us down like drops of water on a stone. The desire of a mother to shield a son, a Black boy, from these dangers provides the specific iconography.

"A Window into Caliban," "A Window into Sycorax," and "A Window into Prospero": These window poems came to me as I thought about the development of these figures as rounded characters. Caliban emerges as the most developed of the figures in the play, in my opinion, at least; he's the one who presents the most interiority. The Johari Window model, in which we see into the character of a person with a 360° view, offered a good model for form. I've found it useful as I developed persona in poems in the past, but this time I left the scaffolding in place.

"Sycorax Blues": I believe there's a story behind the story of Prospero and Sycorax, which would explain his brand of linguistic revenge porn he uses to besmirch her character. Ostensibly—well, one would think, at least that—Prospero has a much bigger issue to deal with back in Milan with his brother Antonio's rise to power over him, but he's somehow just as angry with the inhabitants of this island he's landed on as he should be with his brother. As a result, Prospero decides to terrorize the people of color who were indigenous to the locale, including fighting with a woman who is nowhere in sight. That's bad enough. But he also has an ax to grind specifically against this sista who clearly had power; whose grimoire he must've read; and of whom he wants to erase all memory, which would include her offspring, Caliban. How else can he keep what he's taken? In a case like this, there's usually a history of unrequited love, fear of retaliation, jealousy, envy, or all of the above. When we ask *why is this happening to me?* the most logical answer is often the most obvious one.

"Such Sweet Thunder" sequence: These poems hold some of the magic of *A Midsummer Night's Dream*, but they don't use the plot of the play, just the spirit(s) of it. The "Tailor," in this case, would be the closest thing to a Puck, but he serves no king, other than his willingness to bring young lovers together with his threads. All of these young Malians are actors of a sort—hiding the desires of their hearts from their parents and taking the stage, the dance floor, at night—within the sharp focus of Malick Sidibé's camera.

"When I Waked, I Cried to Dream Again": Yes, this is all fiction; let's get that out of the way, first. It's the question I get asked the most about this one. I wanted to try to capture the feeling of ineffective outrage that builds within us as we obsess over a wrongdoing. What is not a fiction is that I myself often feel powerless as a writer when I hear of yet another tragedy of a life lost through violence, but what haunts me most are the young people who are viewed as a collective threat instead of as a son or a daughter. I've been fortunate to have mentors like Higginbottom, who is a composite of those people, and I've been blessed to avoid being shot when I've had tense encounters with police. When I think about the oral histories we pass down about these encounters—those who have not survived, those who have—the talk we have around our kitchen tables, in barber shops and salons, in our churches and social clubs, I wanted to capture some of that voice here.

"Such Sweet Thunder" poem: Duke Ellington and his orchestra performed at both the 1956 and the 1957 Stratford Shakespeare Festivals, Ontario, Canada. This poem was published in *Poetry Magazine*, and Angela Flores and Lindsay Garbutt started asking questions about details in the poem, which I enjoyed answering because it created a deep dive into the research behind the poem. But Garbutt asked me, "I find that the festival may have been in 1956, not 1957. . . . Do you have a source that says 1957?" And I thought, I sure do, and I was about to take a pic of the album cover and send it to her, but then I thought, *Hmm, where did she see 1956?* It turns out that Ellington performed in 1956 and was invited back to write and perform a suite specific to Shakespeare in 1957. The album *Such Sweet Thunder* is the result of that request. Beyond all that, just listen to this album, which is some of Ellington's most underrated work. I play trombone, and when I hear Britt Woodman do his thing on "Sonnet to Hank Cinq," all I can do is shake my head both in admiration and envy.

"Aaron the Moor": I must admit that I don't really care for *Titus Andronicus* as a play, but I love Aaron the Moor. Sure, the villain-izing of Aaron plays a part in my feeling underwhelmed with the play, but much of my dislike of it is that it's simply an inelegant play. The plot is overwrought with coincidence; the characters aren't very clever and rely on violence to solve—and, ultimately, to complicate—every problem; and Aaron, on the surface, fulfills every Black stereotype both of the late sixteenth century and, sadly, of the twenty-first, as well. But, on further reflection, I see the beauty of Aaron, much in the way I can see through the smoke and mirrors of Prospero to see the sublime in Caliban.

Aaron, in fact, seems to embody the spirit of the blues. His circumstances are fraught, but he copes, he maneuvers, and he even finds ways to reverse his fortune for a while. And when he faces death, he doesn't beg for mercy; he feels justified in his actions in response to his enslavement, and he even brags about his deeds. In other words, Aaron understands that being compliant and complacent won't get him ahead; he's a man ahead of his time.

In that society, the die was cast for his fate, so why should he be a *good Negro*. Written in the late 1500s, the play is a precursor to Queen Elizabeth's edict(s) to evict the Blackamoors from England.

Though England's preoccupation with slavery had already kicked into gear. Like the xenophobia of today, kicking the Black Moors out of England was a sort of *Make [England] Great Again* gesture. As it turns out, our current racial tension is a product of an old racial dialogic campaign, creating a conversation that continues the dynamic exchange we use to define not only our world but also ourselves, which means we have a serious charge: We have to continue raising our voices to break the spell others cast over our bodies.

Acknowledgments

"Aaron the Moor" and "Othello the Moor" appeared in the *Greensboro Review* 112 (Fall 2022).

"Airsoft," "fair," and "Such Sweet Thunder" appeared in *Poetry Magazine*.

"A Tempest in a Teacup" appeared in the Academy of American Poets' Poem-A-Day, https://poets.org/poem/tempest-teacup.

"A Window into Caliban" and "A Window into Sycorax" appeared in *Lampblack Magazine*, 2022 Diaspora Issue.

"Bored, Tamir Chooses to Dream," "Fragments of Tamir's Body," and "Hex" appeared in *The Fight & The Fiddle*, https://fightandfiddle.com/2022/02/04/jordan-poem-2/.

"grandfather" appeared in the *Academy of American Poets' Poem-A-Day*: https://poets.org/poem/grandfather.

"How to Celebrate a Revolution" appeared in *Four Quartets: Poetry in the Pandemic*, eds. Jeffrey Levine and Kristina Marie Darling (North Adams, MA: Tupelo Press, 2020).

The "Such Sweet Thunder" sequence appeared as the chapbook *I Want to See My Skirt*, A. Van Jordan and Cauleen Smith (Greensboro, NC: Unicorn Press, 2021).

"Sycorax Blues" appeared as "A Moment Alone" in the Academy of American Poets' Poem-A-Day, https://poets.org/poem/moment-alone.

"Vestiges" appeared in the Academy of American Poets' Poem-A-Day, https://poets.org/poem/vestiges.

"When I Waked, I Cried to Dream Again," "asterisk," and "suspect" appeared in *StorySouth* (Spring 2022).

The Lannan Foundation made this book possible, and I'm grateful for the work they do and for the work they have done over the years. Both the Lannan Award and the time and space in Marfa, Texas, were transformative for the turning of the mind.

I'd like to thank my editor, Jill Bialosky, both for gently nudging me to show her what I "had been working on" and for her faith in the work. I'd also like to thank Drew Elizabeth Weitman for keeping the trains running on time, Janet McDonald for her keen eye and deep read of the text, and the entire team at W. W. Norton & Co. I'd also like to thank Leslie Shipman and the Shipman Agency.

This book draws extensively upon material preserved and digitized in the Folger Shakespeare Library. I'd particularly like to thank Abbie Weinberg, Research and Reference Librarian.

Most of what sent me to the Folger came from reading the works of scholars and following the breadcrumbs of their paratextual material. For their invaluable scholarship, I'd like to thank Ambereen Dadabhoy; Emily C. Bartels; Errol Hill; Scott Kaiser; Carol Mejia LaPerle; Arthur L. Little Jr.; Jeffrey Masten; the late, elegant Russ McDonald; Noémie Ndiaye; Ian Smith; Ayanna Thompson; Valerie Traub; and Laura Turchi.

I'd like to thank Cauleen Smith not only for our collaboration on *I Want to See My Skirt* but also for permission to use the still images from the film.

I'd like to thank Jack Shainman Gallery, and particularly Jarek Miller, for permission to use Malick Sidibé images in this book.

Thanks to Robin Taylor for her photo of Malick Sidibé's studio in Mali.

I want to thank my dear friend and jazz great Michael Dease for the contemporary soundtrack that I listened to while I wrote this one.

I want to thank my brothers, Cordell Slack and Kenneth Slack, and my wife, Shirley Collado, all of whom keep me loved, supported, and grounded. And thanks to my mother, who, even through the haze of Alzheimer's disease, keeps shining the light. Without my family, I'd be working without a net.

Thanks to Michael Parker not only for being Michael Parker but also for his eyes on the story "When I Waked, I Cried to Dream Again."

Thanks to Sean Singer for reading it all. God bless the eyes of Sean Singer.

I give thanks to the Furious Flower Poetry Center and to Dr. Joanne Gabbin, who lit that flame, and to Lauren K. Alleyne, who keeps it burning, for their early encouragement with these poems.

This one took a long time to write, but I had a lot of encouragement along the way. I'm lucky to have peers who are my heroes: Aaron "the Moor" Coleman, Adrian Matejka, Aisha Sabatini Sloan, Akhil Sharma, Catherine Barnett, C. M. Burroughs, Crystal Williams, Clifford Owens, David Tomas Martinez, Dion Graham, Elizabeth Haukaas, Gabrielle Calvocoressi, Gaurav Desai, Honorée Jeffers, Joel Dias-Porter, Khaled Mattawa, Ladan Osman, Laura Kasischke, Leslie Wingard, Linda Gregerson, Linda Susan Jackson, Lyrae Van Clief-Stefanon, Raymond McDaniel, Rigoberto Gonzalez, Rodney Reyes, Roger Reeves, Sumita Chakraborty, Terrance Hayes, Tommye "Tommyyyeee!" Blount, Tung-Hui Hu, Vievee Francis, and Yona Harvey.

My first reading of these poems was at Bryn Mawr College; thank you Airea Dee Matthews not just for the reading but mostly for the believing, and thanks to Eleanor Wilner and Abby Wender for making the trek out there as I stumbled through the first draft.

Thanks again to Arthur L. Little Jr. for a conversation that sharpened the focus on this project.

And thanks to the Ronin whose brilliance gives me a daily boost of wisdom: Afaa Michael Weaver, Reginald Dwayne Betts, Gregory Pardlo, John Murillo, Major Jackson, Mitchell S. Jackson, Patrick

Rosal, Randall Horton, Tim Seibles, Tyehimba Jess, and Willie Perdomo.

And to my Afrofuturist salon, I'm glad I got to close out the University of Michigan with your brilliance: Ebenezer "Eezer" Agu, Catherine Ventura, Gwendolyn Mugadi, monét cooper, and Sean "Seanie" Civale.

Art Credits